Alexander Graham Bell
BADDECK'S GENTLE GENIUS

Alexander Graham Bell
BADDECK'S GENTLE GENIUS

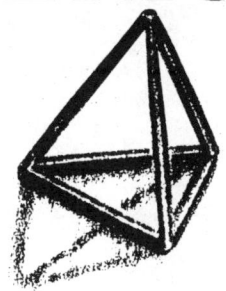

A Portrait by
James B. Lamb

Text copyright © James B. Lamb, 1990, 1998
Illustrations © Kevin Sollows, 1990, 1998

All rights reserved. No part of this book may be reproduced, stored in a retrieval system or transmitted in any form or by any means without the prior written permission from the publisher, or, in the case of photocopying or other reprographic copying, permission from Access Copyright, 1 Yonge Street, Suite 1900, Toronto, Ontario M5E 1E5.

Nimbus Publishing Limited
PO Box 9166
Halifax, NS   B3K 5M8
(902) 455-4286

Printed and bound in Canada

Front cover and interior illustrations: Kevin Sollows

ISBN 0-88999-433-1
First published in 1990 by Lancelot Press
Reprinted in 1998 by Nimbus Publishing

Alexander Graham Bell
BADDECK'S GENTLE GENIUS

In the summer of 1885 Alexander Graham Bell and his family sailed up the Great Bras d'Or in Cape Breton Island, Nova Scotia, on a steamer enroute to Newfoundland, and made a stop at the little village of Baddeck. What was intended as a casual visit grew into an association that was to last for thirty-six years and was to inspire one of the great adventures in the world of science.

Bell was already a world-renowned figure when he arrived at Baddeck, famous as the inventor of the telephone and wealthy as a result of its rapid development into a worldwide communication network. Born in

ALEXANDER GRAHAM BELL

Alexander Graham Bell

Edinburgh, Scotland, in 1847 and, like his father and grandfather before him, a specialist in classifying and correcting problems of speech, he had perfected the Bells' unique system of teaching the deaf to speak correctly. From Scotland, he had moved with his parents to Canada where, in his secret "dreaming place" behind their home at Tutelo Heights, near Brantford, Ontario, he had conceived the notion of making an electrical current vibrate to sound in the same manner as air does, a theory which he would develop through countless experiments culminating in the memorable moment in 1876 when Bell, in his laboratory at Exeter Place, Boston, called out on his primitive telephone to an assistant in the next room: "Mr. Watson, come here; I want to see you." It was the world's first successful telephone call.

Married to a former patient and pupil, Mabel Hubbard, daughter of a wealthy and notable American family and a totally deaf young woman whom he had been able to return to normal social life through his genius, Bell had become a United States citizen and

ALEXANDER GRAHAM BELL

Hand-in-hand with wife about to take a stroll at Beinn Bhreagh.

established residence at Washington in order to take full advantage of the U.S. patents which made his telephone a great commercial success. But he had never really taken to his home in the capital city; the Washington social whirl was distasteful to a man of his solitary habits, and the Washington summer heat was intolerable to a Scot who hankered after the cool grey days and misty rains of his homeland. It was to escape that oppressive heat that he had packed himself, his wife and two daughters, his parents and his in-laws off on a summer visit to Newfoundland, where his father had lived in his youth and where he hoped to find a more congenial climate in which to spend a month or two.

Cape Breton Island and, in particular, Baddeck, had captivated him. The rugged, wooded hills overlooking the deep blue waters of the Bras d'Or had reminded him of the Scottish lochs and highlands; the clear air, sunny days and cool nights were heavenly after the clammy heat of Washington. The names of the places — Barra, Iona, New Campbellton — and of the people —

ALEXANDER GRAHAM BELL

An omnivorous reader, Dr. Bell relaxes in a favorite chair with an early copy of the *National Geographic* magazine.

MacDonald, MacNeil, MacKinnon, MacLeod — were like a breath of Scottish air, and the little village of Baddeck, with its white-painted buildings looking out over a great blue bay and its island-sheltered harbour, seemed enchanting to a refugee from the dusty tumult of the American capital.

When the steamer ran aground enroute to Newfoundland, Bell happily gave up the whole original venture and returned to Baddeck, where, he informed his family, he intended to make his home. He spent the rest of his holiday at the lovely old Telegraph House hotel there, lazing through the sunny days on the broad verandah and the cool nights in a corner bedroom looking out over Baddeck Bay. It was from there that he selected the site for his future home, the beautiful wooded headland of Red Head with the rounded hill above which Bell was to christen "Beinn Bhreagh," Gaelic for "Beautiful Mountain." It was here that he built what was to be his real home for the rest of his life, a marvellous mixture of architectural styles in the Scottish baronial

Alexander Graham Bell

A medley of turrets, balconies and bay windows, Bell's home looks out over the Great Bras d'Or from its hilltop on Red Head.

fashion, encrusted with turrets, balconies, stained glass and ivy-draped stonework, and capable of accommodating up to twenty-six people, in addition to a considerable household staff. It was a remarkable home for a remarkable man, and Bell begrudged every moment he was obliged to spend away from it.

In this imposing castle looking out over a magnificent view, Bell lived, from early spring to late autumn, in unique and colorful style. With his full beard and dressed like a Scottish laird in tweed jacket and knickerbockers above knee-length woollen stockings, he roamed happily about his wooded hilltops, or lazed and read and fished aboard the comfortable houseboat he had built and moored in the sheltered cove. A loving father and a benevolent master, he was the centre of an adoring family and a loyal household of servants, craftsmen, secretaries and scientists, but his habit of working all night, retiring at four in the morning and sleeping late, meant that they often saw all too little of him. A lingering superstition from his Scottish childhood was the dread of "lunacy," thought

A devoted family man all his life, Dr. Bell enjoyed nothing more than a romp with his grandchildren.

in ancient times to be caused by the rays of the moon falling on a sleeper's face, and before retiring on moonlit nights Bell would steal into the bedrooms of his children and, later, grandchildren, to draw the curtains that kept out the moonbeams.

Apart from these midnight visits, the festive family dinners, which often ended with singing or piano performances, were the only times which Bell could spare for the family life he loved, when he was working hard on some project. And projects there were in plenty to occupy the teeming mind of one of the world's greatest inventors. Almost everything interested him, and at one time or another he considered in passing, or applied himself in depth, to concepts varying from sheep breeding to radar, from phonograph recording to thought transference, from distilling freshwater from the sea to hydrophones and sonar. When President Garfield was shot, Bell invented an induction probe to search for the bullet lodged deep within the wound; when an infant son died of a breathing defect he developed an 'iron lung.'

Alexander Graham Bell

Alexander Graham Bell in his study.

One of his most remarkable developments was the tetrahedron, a cell shape based on equilateral triangles and lighter and stronger than rectangular construction or the arch, which he was to use subsequently in the building of many of his projects, from kites to a giant steel observation tower on the top of Beinn Bhreagh.

But throughout his long lifetime the great inventor's dominant interest lay in communication, and the projects which occupied most of his time were concerned with the transference of ideas and of people; concepts like an automatic telephone exchange and the heavier-than-air flying machine.

His working habits varied according to the stage of development of the project. An abstainer from alcohol, he was a heavy smoker of pipes and cigars, and might spend long hours alone in his study, wreathed in tobacco smoke, interrupted, especially on the windy nights he loved, with long walks over the hills. At other times he would spend night after night in a cluttered construction shed or

Workmen run for cover as an immense tetrahedral kite plummets from the sky.

laboratory tinkering with some model, sometimes sucking in his breath in exasperation when something failed to work and hissing the only exclamation of annoyance he allowed himself: 'Geethe! Geethe! Geethe!'

When visited by other distinguished men of science, as he often was, he might sit all night with his guest on a verandah overlooking the sea, their cigars glowing in the darkness as they discussed some problem of mutual concern.

One such discussion, about the possibility of exerting force against air, led to a consideration of the notion that a cat, dropped in any position, always landed on its feet. To do so it must somehow exert leverage against the air, it was decided, but a practical test was necessary. Bell's staff was promptly enlisted to round up all three cats in the household establishment and, because Bell was a gentle man who would never dream of causing pain to any helpless animal, several mattresses were stripped from their beds and gathered in a pile below the verandah rail. At a given signal, a

Alexander Graham Bell

gardener dropped each cat, upside down, one after the other from a window overhead, while the great inventor and his guest, both notable men of science, craned forward to watch each animal landing on the piled-up mattresses. All three landed on their feet and scuttled away into the darkness without any hurt save to dignity. It was a demonstration of the most convincing kind; leverage *could* be exerted against thin air. The two men settled back, satisfied, into their verandah chairs and resumed their discussion and the enjoyment of their cigars.

Increasingly, Bell turned his attention to the problems of manned flight through the air. The future, he was convinced, lay with a heavier-than-air machine rather than with the various types of lighter-than-air balloons which were already common throughout the world, and which had inherent problems regarding safety from fire and explosion, from temperature and tempest, and above all, of control in anything save ideal conditions. In 1896 Bell began dreaming of experiments which might be undertaken with kites to solve

Family and neighbours, old and young, join Bell in helping tow a huge wedge-shaped kite aloft on a windy hilltop.

the problems of heavier-than-air flight and in 1898 he began to build his first large kites, using the tetrahedron type of cellular construction which he had just perfected. The big kites were built with black spruce frames and red silk surfaces by the skilled staff of craftsmen he had assembled at Beinn Bhreagh, and an enormous wooden shed, 'the Kite House,' was built on the shore of Baddeck Bay to house them.

Side by side with his kite experiments to probe the problems of lifting weight aloft in the air, Bell worked tirelessly on the matter of propulsion.

He experimented with a primitive helicopter, driven by steam jets on the rotor tips, and in his search for lightweight sources of power he experimented with gunpowder rockets, with spectacular but disappointing results. Eventually he concluded that a variation of the screw propeller, so successful in the propulsion of modern steamships, could provide the only practical means of propelling an aircraft and thenceforth a succession of wooden propellers, each more sophisticated

ALEXANDER GRAHAM BELL

Bell (at right) and workmen watch as a giant ring kite lifts off from a summer meadow at Beinn Bhreagh.

and efficient than its predecessor, were turned out by Beinn Bhreagh craftsmen.

Meanwhile the Bell kites grew ever larger and more complex, and their lifting power so great that large numbers of men with ropes were required to launch and control them. The great inventor himself loved nothing better than to take hold of a rope on a windswept hilltop and, with a long line of friends, family, workers and neighbours, haul one of his huge red silk contraptions up into the clouds. They were large and complicated enough now to bear names, and not merely experiment numbers; the 'Diones' (Bird of Omen) had a great hinged tail and a pendulum system of flight control, and in December, 1905, Bell successfully launched the monster 'Frost King' which, with its vast array of 1300 red silk cells, had such lifting power that it accidentally lifted a 165-pound workman thirty feet into the air at the end of a rope. Neil MacDermid of Baddeck thus inadvertently became the first man to be taken aloft in a Bell kite. He would not be the last.

In the early years of the 20th century

ALEXANDER GRAHAM BELL

Age and youth confer together; Dr. Bell and Casey Baldwin inspect preparations for a flight of the Silver Dart.

aerial flight had become a worldwide obsession. Everywhere, experimental aircraft were coming nearer and nearer to fulfilling their inventors' dreams; Bell's Boston friend, Samuel Langley, had flown a steam-powered model aeroplane (or 'aerodrome,' as he and Bell referred to their aircraft), and two midwesterners, Orville and Wilbur Wright, by December, 1903, had managed to actually fly their machine a few feet above the ground for a short distance, which encouraged others by showing that at least it could be done. Bell now became aware of the need for other brains, other hands, to work along with his in trying to solve the many problems posed by heavier-than-air flight, and accordingly he began to look about him for bright young engineers.

In Baddeck he found young Douglas McCurdy, son of a friend of Bell's, and in the fall of 1906 McCurdy brought home from the University of Toronto another of his graduating class of engineers, Fred Baldwin, nicknamed 'Casey' after 'Casey at the Bat,' because of his athletic prowess. A handsome, charming and brilliant young man, captain of

Alexander Graham Bell

All for one and one for all; the Aerial Experiment Association in session on the steps of Beinn Bhreagh. Left to right: Glen Curtiss, Lieutenant Thomas Selfridge, Dr. Bell, Casey Baldwin and J.A.D. McCurdy.

the famous 1905 Varsity Blues championship football team, Casey was exactly the assistant Bell had been looking for. Casey came to Beinn Bhreagh for a two-week vacation, and stayed for a lifetime.

As rumours of the exciting developments at Baddeck spread abroad, other young men interested in experimental flight drifted in to the Bell workshops, and a few of the more promising were invited to stay. And in the fall of 1907, at the prompting of his wife Mabel, Bell formed an association without precedent in the world of science.

Called 'The Aerial Experiment Association,' it bound together for the period of one year a diverse group of brilliant and enthusiastic young men; Glen Curtiss, a dour but gifted engine-maker from Hammondsport, New York; Thomas Selfridge, a United States Army lieutenant; McCurdy, Baldwin and Bell. All were pledged to devote a year of working life to the project, with Bell providing laboratory space and building facilities, and Mabel furnishing the necessary working capital. Each member undertook to build a

J.A.D. McCurdy, at the wheel of the *Silver Dart*, first flew from the ice of Baddeck Bay on February 23, 1909

prototype machine of his own, and to assist the others in finishing and launching theirs. The young men met before a roaring fire in Beinn Bhreagh's baronial surroundings and toasted their new undertaking. It was not so much a business enterprise they were embarking on, as a kind of purposeful brotherhood; like D'Artagnan and the Three Musketeers, it was to be 'one for all, and all for one,' and it marked the beginning of the most remarkable adventure in the annals of Canadian science.

The first craft to be finished and tested was the 'Cygnet,' Bell's largest and most sophisticated kite, designed to carry a man aloft and to be, to some extent at least, controlled by him. This vast tetrahedral glider had its 3,400 red silk cells framed with duraluminium for extra strength. Far too heavy to be launched in the normal way from some windswept hilltop, the great machine was taken out onto the whitecapped Bras d'Or waters on a barge, and then towed aloft by the steamer *Bluehill*, running at full speed into a twenty-five knot wind. With the intrepid Tom

Alexander Graham Bell

Selfridge at the controls, the enormous structure rose as easily and gracefully as a bird, and climbed swiftly to a height of 168 feet, a record altitude for a manned heavier-than-air craft, where the 175-pound Lieutenant Selfridge levelled her off. Cygnet flew serenely along at the end of her tow line for more than seven minutes when, the wind dropping, she descended as her pilot brought her down gracefully to the surface of the water. Unfortunately Selfridge, from his cramped position in the centre of the huge machine, could not get a clear view beneath him nor feel when his pontoons touched the water, while the view of the watchers on the *Bluehill* was momentarily obscured by a cloud of smoke from the steamer's funnel. As a result the towline was not slipped from 'Cygnet,' nor cut loose from the ship, so that the fragile craft was towed some way through rough water and disintegrated. Selfridge himself popped to the surface unhurt and full of enthusiasm for the flight he had accomplished, the first manned and controlled flight by a Bell kite.

ALEXANDER GRAHAM BELL

The great man's favorite retreat, Dr. Bell's houseboat ended its days propped up on a nearby beach.

Baddeck's Gentle Genius

But Bell had been obsessed with the need for stability; ideally he considered an aeroplane should be able to hover just above the ground if need be, and land at walking speeds. In roundtable discussion, the young men of the A.E.A. decided that simple wings, with less air resistance than the unwieldy kites, must be the way of the future, and Bell now concurred. Each of the adventurers set to work on his own design and discussed those of their associates, pooling their brains to solve their problems and spurred on by reports from Kittyhawk, New Jersey, and elsewhere, which showed both that heavier-than-air flight was possible and that much had to be done to make it a practical proposition.

In the winter of 1907-8, operations moved temporarily to the Hammondsport home of Curtiss in the hope of milder weather, and it was from the frozen lake there that Selfridge's 'Red Wing' was flown a hundred yards at a height of ten feet by Baldwin, elected as pilot in Selfridge's absence (the army called) as the only man in the party not on skates! Baldwin's own machine, named 'White Wing' for its

ALEXANDER GRAHAM BELL

The Silver Dart lifts off from Baddeck Bay, the first aircraft to fly in the British Empire.

white fabric covering, the group having at last run out of red silk, was next aloft, covering a thousand feet with the aid of its new 'warped wingtips,' later called ailerons. Glen Curtiss then took his 'June Bug,' its fabric painted with a clear substance they called 'dope,' up in July, 1908, and flew it more than a kilometer to win a trophy put up by a science magazine.

But by all odds the most successful machine of all was McCurdy's siver-painted 'Silver Dart,' first flown from the ice of Baddeck Bay on February 23, 1909. It maintained an average speed of forty miles an hour and covered a distance of half a mile, and was subsequently flown on ever-longer flights culminating in one of more than twenty miles.

With the 'Silver Dart,' the A.E.A. had made heavier-than-air flight demonstrably a practical proposition; with its flight, the first ever by a Canadian and indeed the first ever in the British Empire, the Air Age had arrived in Canada, an era that was to change the face of the nation and make possible the opening up of vast areas hitherto inaccessible.

On the evening of March 31, 1909, the

Alexander Graham Bell

young aviators met again before the great fireplace of Beinn Bhreagh to dissolve their partnership; the Aerial Experiment Association, its operations successful, had run its appointed course. It was an emotional parting; one of their members, Thomas Selfridge, had been killed a few months before in the crash of a plane piloted by Orville Wright, and the others were going their separate ways. Curtis, assisted by McCurdy, founded the large aircraft firm that still bears his name. Standing with the great inventor, a sort of father-figure to them all, the young men shook hands with deep feeling; it was the end of a great adventure, the most memorable time of their lives, and all were conscious of having helped to shape the future history of the world.

But for Bell and Baldwin, a new adventure was about to begin. For the aging inventor, young Casey had become almost the son he never had; both the Bell male children had died as infants. Baldwin had drive, energy, a quick mind and the perseverance which the older man needed, as well as the tact and

Alexander Graham Bell

In clouds of spray and tongues of flame, the giant hydrofoil HD4 thunders down Baddeck Bay with Casey Baldwin and Dr. Bell aboard.

understanding which helped him appreciate the flashes of Bell genius while discarding the irrelevancies which sometimes distracted the course of the great man's thought.

Ever since 1906, when he had first sketched a possible model, Bell had been preoccupied by the notion of a hydrofoil, a machine which could fly on planes through the water in the same way an aircraft flies through air. He had been impressed by a visit, during one of his frequent tours about the world, with the Italian inventor Enrico Forlanini who was experimenting with just such a device and, finding Baldwin enthusiastic, he set about designing his own hydrofoil.

It was the beginning of an adventure that, particularly for young Baldwin, was to be every bit as exciting and demanding as the struggle to fly. With Casey doing the bulk of the work and Bell assisting with the advice made priceless by his genius and experience, the partners launched their first machine, HD (for hydrodome) One, in the fall of 1911. Small and primitive as it was, it flashed across the water at fifty miles an hour on a number of

Journey's end; Mabel and Dr. Bell in the last days at Beinn Bhreagh.

Baddeck's Gentle Genius

runs before coming to grief and crashing into the shore in 1912. Its successor, HD-Two, a sort of stubby-winged affair, was a complete failure, while the somewhat more successful HD-Three embarrassed everyone by turning turtle, capsizing in dramatic fashion after striking a wave during a demonstration for the Prince of Monaco, visiting Baddeck in his yacht.

But the fourth and final model, HD-4, was the hydrofoil that Baldwin and Bell had dreamed of. Her long, cigar-shaped hull was borne well clear of the water at speed, so that it rode above the surface, borne up on the angled horizontal planes of her trellis-like foils fore and aft. Her performance at first limited by the inadequate engines then available, HD-4 came into her own on September 9, 1919, when, powered by two enormous 350 hp Liberty aero engines, each trailing a six-foot tongue of flame from the exhausts, and with Casey Baldwin, cap on backwards and muffled in a coonskin coat, huddled at the huge wheel, she roared down the still waters of Baddeck Bay in a cloud of flying spray at speeds of more than

Alexander Graham Bell

seventy miles an hour. It was the fastest man had ever travelled on water, a record that stunned a basically horse-and-buggy world and was to stand for years. The Bell-Baldwin adventure had been crowned with spectacular success!

But time was running out for the partnership of the aging genius and the brilliant young engineer. Bell was well into his seventies when the HD-4 set its world water speed mark, and although the brain was as active as ever, his store of physical energy was running out. Always a big, heavy man, he began to lose weight and to tire ever more easily. In 1922 he took out patents on certain aspects of hydrofoil design, the last patents of a long and inventive lifetime.

As his energies flagged, so he began to spend ever longer periods among the idyllic surroundings and cool air of the Cape Breton home he had come to love more than any place else on earth. It was there, in the early hours of August 2, 1922, that the end came. Sitting at his bedside, his hand in hers, his devoted wife Mabel felt the life ebbing from the great man.

ALEXANDER GRAHAM BELL

The great man is laid to rest atop his Beautiful Mountain, watched by mourning family, staff, and neighbours.

Leaning forward, she kissed him and whispered: 'Don't leave me!'

Gently but firmly, she felt the response; Bell's last message as he slipped from the mortal world. It was the word in the hand language he had devised for his deaf wife; the pressure of his fingers saying 'No.'

Bell was buried on the top of his Beautiful Mountain, looking out over the Great Bras d'Or, to be joined shortly by his grieving wife, who died only five months later, their tomb marked by simple inscriptions on a rugged boulder. Casey Baldwin, the Canadian boy whom they had loved as a son, died there in 1948 and lies in a small cemetery nearby. In the intervening years the handful of 'magnificent young men' who had planned their flying machines before the log fires of Beinn Bhreagh, all died, one by one, in varying places and circumstances.

Their great adventure was over, but the memories of the days when they filled the sky with huge kites, sent tiny cloth-covered contraptions darting into the air of wintry afternoons or roared through the morning mists of Baddeck Bay in a great grey cigar, wreathed in flame and spray; these memories live on today in Baddeck.

The big old house is still filled each summer with the offspring of generations of Bell descendants; nearby a museum preserves and displays the many and varied creations of one of the world's most inventive minds.

But the true legacy of Alexander Graham Bell lies in a world linked by the telephone and the aeroplane, a world in which the deaf may 'hear' and the mute may 'speak,' thanks to the genius of the gentle patriarch who loved to walk abroad on dark and windy nights through the woods and fields of Beinn Bhreagh, his beloved Beautiful Mountain.